Introduction

Following are a number of brief discussions on a wide variety of self improvement topics. Most of the information comes from more than thirty years of business experience. The discussions provide information that I have found helpful in improving my own life. They are not meant to be all inclusive, but they help provide you with an outline of how to improve various areas of your life to make you more focused, more productive and a more efficient employee or manager.

In Memory of my daughter Michelle
(1993-2014)
A unique inspiring person,
who was taken from us too soon.
Thank you for giving me the courage and
inspiration to write.

Contents

Consistency 5

Employee Value...7

Staying Positive - It Is All About You.................................9

Keeping Your Work Ethic Fine Tuned 12

Communication - The Lost Art 14

So How Do I Discuss a Difficult Topic at Work?...............16

6 Tips On Discussing Difficult Personal Topics During the Holiday Season..18

So it's the New Year - Now What?......................................20

Staying Connected to Your Network Through LinkedIn 22

Why Do Good Things Always Happen In Threes?.........................24

Use Your Day Wisely..30

Are Expectations Controlling Your Life or Guiding Your Life? 35

Staying Current in a World of Change................................38

Do Rituals Rule Our Lives? 45

A Good Employee - The Right Fit at the Right Time 47

What's to Worry About...50

Finesse Equals Success...52

Did Dinosaurs Have Souls?...54

Ever Try Some "People Centric" Behavior?..............57

Where's Your Moral Compass 59

Take Time To Challenge Your Life 61

Spend a Weekend Reaching for Relaxation............63

Let Laughter Rule Your Day 65

Who's Keeping Time Anyway? 67

What's It Like Being Lucky? 70

Business Etiquette in the Technology Age..............72

Consistency

Consistency in the workplace will allow you to be more efficient and make you a more productive worker. Plus by completing work tasks in less time who knows, maybe you'll have time to take up a new hobby like clock repair.

1. Don't procrastinate. This may seem like a simple statement, but anything that can be done today can and should be done today.

2. Understand your energy patterns. You know what times of the day and week you are most productive. Use those times to do more complicated tasks. Schedule less complicated tasks for those times when your energy levels are low or fellow group or employee members are unavailable.

3. Be consistent in your handling of all correspondence that crosses your desk. The less times you handle a piece of information the more quickly and efficiently you can keep tasks moving forward.

4. Add time to network or to increase your knowledge base. This includes staying on top of latest trends. Think of yourself as an information hub. The more information and connections you have the more relevant and valuable you are to your employer and prospective customers and business associates.

5. Follow through in the same manner when dealing with new customers or contacts. Having the steps written down will allow you to handle each person with the same level of attention and detail.

6. Thank you cards or thank you notes are always a must. It's always a nice added touch.

7. Try to offer something of value to a current or prospective customer. It can be a simple tip or piece of useful information, or some easy way you can help them out now or in the future.

8. Always follow up. if you say you are going to do something, do it. Give them a time frame. Keep the person advised. if you know something you are doing won't be completed on time let the person know as soon as possible and give them a revised time frame. Never keep customers in the dark.

Follow these steps and you'll find you'll sleep better at night and wake up refreshed wanting to face the new work day. These are just my personal observations based on my own workplace experiences. Incorporate and use this advice at your own risk.

Employee Value

Creating value for your employer is important. Eight tips I've learned over the years.

1.   Scalability – You need to know the details. Be able to handle all different parts of your job related tasks not just oversee the management of them. You become more valuable when you are able to do hands on work when needed. You will also have a better understanding of the entire work process.

2.   Adaptability – With constant changes in technology you need to be able to adapt to new ways of doing things and be open to new ideas. Always be ready to embrace change in your work environment.

3.   Self Improvement - Always strive to increase your knowledge base by taking seminars or attending classes. Think of yourself as an information hub The information you have at your disposal the more valuable you become.

4.   Soft Skills – Think about ways to improve how you interact with co workers in the office and with customers. Try to get feedback from others on how they perceive your interaction with them in different situations. Work on maintaining consistent and timely communications in the office.

5.   Work with Diverse Groups – Our world is getting more global and more diverse every day. Think about joining a group outside of your age group, ethnicity, or cultural background. It's all about learning how to interact and communicate with new and different types of people.

6.   Stay Connected – Stay in touch with people you've

met through different jobs or groups. It doesn't have to be on a weekly basis. Just make sure you touch base with them from time to time.

7.   Be Relevant – You don't need to be the center of the office discussion, but make sure you are in the loop and comment on issues that are within your field of expertise. Let your employer know what knowledge you have and what you are available to contribute.

8.   Positive Attitude – Stay positive. Charles Swindoll said Life is 10 % of what happens to you and 90 % how you react to it. Use your 90 % wisely.

Staying Positive - It Is All About You

Recently some articles have come out that suggest that negative people might just be wired differently, that they have a predisposition towards negativity[1]. Whether or not we have a predisposition to a positive or negative outlook, I like to think that we can all vary where we want to be on the continuum of positive vs. negative. On any given day depending on what events we face or how we feel we move along the negative/positive line and find a spot to sit for that day. We make a choice whether we choose to interact with that day negatively or positively. Here are some tips on how to set a positive direction for the day.

1. Prepare for the next day the night before. If there are any loose odds and ends you can get out of the way the night before do them. Charge your cell phone, decide what you're going to wear the next day, put your handbag or brief case by the door, and write down notes to yourself on any tasks or errands you need to get done by the end of the day. This reduces distractions in the morning.

2. You set the tone for the day. Look in the mirror in the morning and say out loud "Today is going to be a great day!".

3. Understand what can create negative situations for you. Decide in advance how you will handle those situations. Be prepared for angry customers, difficult family member discussions, and negative people you might come in contact with during the day. Then, mentally note how you will work through those

---

[1] http;//www.earthtimes.org/health/optimistic-people-wired-differently/1497/

situations in a positive manner in advance. The positive attitude you present can help craft a more positive outcome in any situation.

4.   Set a morning routine. Maybe it includes reading the paper, having a cup of coffee, doing a cross word puzzle, or exercise. A regular routine, grounds you for the day and relaxes your mind putting it in the right frame to start the day.

5.   Don't let events negatively impact your overall mental attitude. You can't determine what events you might encounter during the day, but you can decide how you will respond. Look at every event as a learning experience and do your best to handle it in the best positive way possible. An interesting article to think about is "Why People Remember Negative Events More Than Positive Ones"[2].

6.   Set something to do at the end of the day to unwind and let your brain relax. Meditate, exercise, unwind in low key conversation, make a casual dinner. You need "you" time to relax and recharge.

7.   Eat right and get regular sleep. This gives your mind and body the basis for maintaining a positive outlook.

---

[2] www.nytimes.com/2012/03/24/your-money/why-people-remember-negative-events-more-than-positive-ones.html

Stay positive, enjoy the week and remember staying positive is all about you. Want some additional ideas on how to stay positive, go to the following articles:

http://blog.bufferapp.com/how-to-rewire-your-brains-for-positivity-and-happiness

http://successify.net/2012/10/31/22-things-happy-people-do-differently

Keeping Your Work Ethic Fine Tuned

Why are people afraid to talk about work ethic these days? You still need to tell a young kid fresh out of high school that they need to put in their time, work hard, and pay their dues to get ahead; that easy money doesn't really come easy and that there is always a catch if it comes too easy. I'm not sure how the nature/nurture principle applies here. But, I do wonder whether you can instill a work ethic into someone who doesn't currently have it. For me, I ask myself five questions to help me assess whether I am working at maintaining a strong work ethic.

1. Am I striving for good or great work ethic? This is about my inner energy level to get things done. Am I maintaining self motivation at a high enough level to work hard at what I do, understand what is expected of me, and follow through to completion?

2. Do I have "attitude" or "can do"? There is a big difference between a person with a negative attitude and a person who positively accepts new tasks. People with a strong work ethic have a positive attitude. They don't shy away from new tasks, but look at them as a challenge to solve a problem. Never say "no". If you say no, you have already closed the door on a new opportunity or learning experience.

3. Do I give extra effort or enough effort? I shouldn't accept something less than perfection in what I do. While I can't be perfect, I should strive to go the extra mile in what I'm doing, taking extra effort to make sure a task is done right the first time.

4. Am I always learning or do I already know enough? I need to maintain my innate curiosity and always want to learn more. New ideas and new information allow my mind to stay in top form and gives me fresh tools to better handle my daily work functions. I should never be afraid to improve my understanding of the world around me.

5. Do I ask "Why me?" or "Why not me?" I should never say "Why me?" Instead, I should always be ready and prepared to accept any challenge that comes my way. By positively saying, "Why not me?" I embrace the possibility that I'm up for any challenge and can get things done.

What work ethic do you present to those around you? Can you learn to improve upon your current work ethic? Always challenge yourself to improve. Don't be afraid to ask yourself is my current work ethic as strong as it should be.

Communication - The Lost Art

Now with all the electronic gadgets taking up our time and distracting us we need to give more effort communicating with one another for our communications to be effective. Texting, e-mailing, and other forms of electronic communication have transformed how we communicate, making our communicating less personal. Yet, on average we spend 70 to 80 percent of our time communicating[3]. Following are some thoughts on how we can get the most out of communicating with others.

1. Know your audience. Make sure you have their attention, that they are listening and not distracted; communicate in a format that is friendly to them – using texting or e-mailing in place of face to face contact might work better with certain age groups; use words that are mutually understandable; choose your words wisely, make sure the industry jargon you use is understood by the other person. Something to think about is an article on communication tips[4].

2. Talking isn't communicating. Communicating is all about interacting with another person. Make sure you are interacting with the other person. Talk, but take time to listen. Look for the message the other person is trying to deliver to you as well. Remember, communication is a two way street. There are certain nonverbal cues to look for[5].

3. Make sure there is a meeting of the minds. The

---

[3] http://extension.missouri.edu/p/CM150
[4] http://www.huffingtonpost.com/nancy-colier/communication-tips_b_3856199.html
[5] http://www.helpguide.org/articles/relationships/nonverbal-communication.htm

same words mean different things to different people. Make sure you are both on the same page. A good article on this discusses the difference between literal and abstract thinkers[6].

4. Defining expectations is important. Determine in advance what you are expecting to happen with the communication. Is the communication intended to be personal or business related? Are you just expressing your opinion? Do you want someone to take action? Are you looking for information? If the communication is beyond a personal conversation you may want to plan and outline the communication in advance.

5. Simple steps to communicating. A Simple rule of thumb for any communication is - tell people what you will tell them; tell them; tell them what you told them. Make sure to state your ideas concisely; get a verbal response to resolve any misconceptions; make sure you've reached a mutual understanding; and always be willing to follow up and clarify as needed.

Not everyone communicates in the same way you do. In order to communicate effectively you need to meet people on their terms – communicate with them in their favorite mode of communication as much as possible. You may not think of communication as an art, but next time before you communicate with someone, take an extra moment and think about how you actually will do it. Communication is all about mutual interaction and understanding.

---

[6] http://blog.brazencareerist.com/2010/03/09/the-hardest-part-of-communications-literal-thinkers-vs-abstract-thinkers/

So How Do I Discuss a Difficult Topic at Work?

We've all been there. How do we begin to discuss a difficult topic? To make it more difficult, many times personal and business issue overlap. In this post we will cover difficult business conversations. Here are some points to follow to make the whole process go more smoothly:

1. Is it a business related issue? Don't try to turn a personal issue into a business issue. Attempting to control personal choices, where company policy doesn't cover or regulate employee conduct can lower employee morale and can lead to legal issues. Before moving forward with a discussion, review your employee handbook or talk to your HR department. It's better to be safe than sorry.

2. Are you the appropriate person to have the discussion? Make sure you are the right person to discuss the issue, given your business relationship with the other person. Is there another more direct supervisor or a supervisor with a closer working relationship that might be better suited to discuss the issue with   the employee?

3. Keep the discussion on a strictly business level. This can be even harder with small businesses where personal and business issues are more likely to overlap. If there are business and personal issues intertwined, clarify how the issues affect the business side of things. For example if you are raising a   concern about proper attire, keep the discussion on how the employee's attire affects customer perception and company policy. Don't judge that person on a personal level. Personal issues should stay personal, make it clear whether the issue you are discussing is a company business related matter or only

a personal recommendation.

4. Discuss the topic on terms that will make the other person feel comfortable. It isn't about your comfort level it's about their comfort level. Don't profess to understand exactly what that person is thinking or feeling. Keep the discussion focused, short and to the point. Simple statements will tend to take emotions out of the discussion. With that being said speak in a manner and tone you would want to be spoken to.

5. Say something sooner rather than later. By waiting a situation tends to fester. It won't just go away because you aren't talking about it.

6. Do you have all the facts? Don't discuss based on assumptions. Only discuss as far as you know is fact. Once you say something you can't take it back, so be careful what you say.

7. Follow up after the initial discussion. Don't belabor the initial discussion, but if there are additional things that need to be followed up on do it in a timely manner.

A good article on dealing with difficult topics provides you with tips on having difficult situations[7].

Dealing with difficult topics is all about keeping the discussion timely, relevant, and focused, and doing it with respect for the other the person.

---

[7] hbr.org/web/management-tip/tips-on-having-difficult-conversations

6 Tips On Discussing Difficult Personal Topics During the Holiday Season

Discussing difficult personal topics is all about understanding boundaries and addressing those topics in a way that doesn't offend the other person. Keep in mind that personal topics can easily spill into business relationships, so tread lightly as not to ruin an ongoing business relationship. Following are some points to keep in mind:

1. Do you really want to go there? Make sure it is a topic that really needs to be discussed. Some topics might be important to you, but won't produce a positive outcome. For example, if your friend always shows up late for meetings, it might be appropriate to start a discussion to clear the air. However, if you don't like the wardrobe choices your friend makes, as long as the clothes are clean and situation appropriate, you probably don't want to address the topic.

2. Set the right tone before starting the discussion. This is true with any discussion. Open up the discussion positively. Start with a cordial introduction and show personal interest in the other person by asking them about what they have been up to. Never start off with the difficult topic first. Choose a relaxed atmosphere and place.

3. Choose words wisely. Don't use words with double meanings or complex words. Use words that are exact and to the point. Instead of using phrases like "you're overbearing" or "you're obtuse" use phrases like "you have a forceful or direct personality" and "In some

situations you're slow to perceive the situation . . . ."

4. Keep any personal judgments out of the discussion. Present the topic using factual not emotional perceptions. Use just enough forcefulness to get your point across, but don't be overly pushy. It's up to them to take your advice not you to force it on them.

   Use positive reinforcement. If you can, present the topic in a positive light. For example stating "When you're in a group, it's great to ask questions, it shows you are interested in what others have to say.", creates a more positive spin, than saying "You should really stop talking about yourself all the time, it gets old really fast."

   Be prepared to listen and take counter comments. Most people don't like receiving personal criticism. Be prepared for the unexpected. You can't always anticipate how people will respond. They may challenge your assessment or they may counter with a personal comment about you. Whatever the response is, stay calm, keep eye contact, make it clear that you are trying to give them helpful insight, and be prepared to disengage from the topic of discussion if necessary.

Remember make sure to set your boundaries, keep your topic discussion positively focused and be prepared to listen. Your goal is to keep that friend for life not to distance them from you. Handled correctly, the discussion can leave you both with a stronger bond.

So it's the New Year - Now What?

The New Year arrives and suddenly everything is supposed to be different. All the old problems, whether they are solved or not, and all those character shortcomings have been left behind with the start of the New Year. The holidays were perfect, harried get togethers with distant relatives and last minute gift shopping excluded. You're starting with a clean slate. And this year you've made those 10 perfect resolutions so the year is guaranteed to run smoothly. Before we get to more realistic resolutions for the New Year:

1. First, throw out those resolutions you've jotted down. Have you ever followed through with any of them for any year you can remember? Can you even find your old resolutions?

2. Stop kidding yourself about starting up your exercise routine five days a week because you've started up a membership at the local fitness club and want to lose a few holiday pounds. Fitness clubs make a large part of annual revenues in January due to the after holiday rush, come February it's back to the same old crowd at the fitness club.

3. Don't make sweeping resolutions that tend to make your life more stressful and open yourself up to instances when they can't be met. You don't need resolutions like I will not be late to any more meetings, I won't procrastinate, and I will change my car oil every 5000 miles.

Instead make a shorter more general, more adaptable resolution list:

1. Stay positive. You decide how you approach what happens to you on a daily, weekly and monthly basis.

2. Look at what areas you are already happy with in your life and see if you can build on those. Are there hobbies that you enjoy doing, but haven't found the time to do? Make time to do your yoga, cycling, cooking, or writing.

3. Don't try to make drastic changes overnight, start with small ones.

4. Set up to make one change a month for each month during the entire year.

5. Ask yourself - What do you really need to change? Change isn't always necessary; consistency in how you live your life can be a better approach.

6. Don't take on the hardest change first. Baby steps sometimes lead to big changes over time.

7. Rather than saying, "I can't wait for this year to end", say "I'm too busy living in this year for it to end".

See, now instead of a list of rigid resolutions you have an outline to reuse every year. Remember, years aren't measured by the number of days but by how you choose to fill each one of those days. Enjoy your new year.

Staying Connected to Your Network Through LinkedIn

LinkedIn is a great way to stay connected with your business network. The nice thing about it is that it doesn't take much time. Just a half hour a week and you can stay connected. Following are the basics on getting started:

1. Setting up your account is easy. Go to www.LinkedIn.com and create an account.

2. Next, over time you can create your profile. You don't need to do it all at once. Look at a sample profile - http://www.linkedin.com/profile/sample.

3. Once you've created your account and filled in your profile, you can add new connections a few different ways:

   (a) Simply search for individual names using the search function[8].

   (b) Join one of the many groups. Look for groups under the Interests tab. One local state group worth joining is Linked Minnesota.

   (c) Follow the college you attended by looking under Education in the Interests tab. Then you can search for other Alumni you may know.

   (d) Once you've started to build your connections work on staying noticed. Depending on how you set your settings, updates will appear on your home page (Need help with settings and understanding updates, go to the help page on LinkedIn[9]). These are updates from different connections you have added or groups or companies you follow. Feel free to add comments or add a simple "Like" if you like

---

[8] http://blog.linkedin.com/2013/03/25/linkedin-search-just-got-smarter/
[9] http://help.linkedin.com/app/home/

the update. Congratulate people on anniversaries or job changes.

(e) As you get more comfortable add your own updates. Once a week is fine. It keeps your name out there.

For a look at the statistics on how most people use LinkedIn you can look at the popular ways people use LinkedIn[10].

For more ideas on how to use LinkedIn go to "Five LinkedIn Strategies You Haven't Thought of Before"[11].

You don't need to overdo it. Just set a specific amount of time per week to manage your LinkedIn account. You can even access LinkedIn through your smart phone using free apps[12].

---

[10]http://www.ragan.com/Main/Articles/The_mostpopular_ways_people_use_LinkedIn_47070.aspx

[11] http://www.forbes.com/sites/cherylsnappconner/2013/10/27/five-linkedin-strategies-you-havent-thought-of-before/

[12] http://help.linkedin.com/app/home/

Why Do Good Things Always Happen In Threes?

Where did we ever come up with the idea that good things and bad things all happen in threes. How do we really decide what's good enough to count as "good" or bad enough to count as "bad". Those distant relatives that visited and decided to stay with you a week, is that good or bad. If they decide to head home early is that good, especially if they are your spouse's relatives? Or, can we only count good or bad things that occur totally unexpectedly. The origin that good or bad things happen in a set number goes back to ancient times. Depending on the culture, the total number is different. (For more background on this go to - "The Three Rule: Superstition or Ominous Part of Our History?"[13]

So getting back to my initial point, why do we want to set a limit on the number of good or bad things that happen to us in the foreseeable future?

It's really all about setting a time frame for closure so that we can move on to the next segment of our life. We don't like the idea of uncertainty and we always crave a sense of control. Even though we can't control whether something good or bad will happen to us we want to feel that once something happens to us we can know with certainty what we can expect going forward; that there will be some finality to what type of events will happen to us in the near future.

What does this say about human nature? It really says we are continually trying to define what types of things are

---

[13] http://articles.philly.com/1997-09-10/news/25550256_1_princess-diana-phillies-culture

within our control and what types are out of our control. We are just trying to add one more item to the list of those things within our control. What can we learn about this?

1. Work to understand what pieces of your life are in your control and work at improving how you positively deal with those pieces. Some of the things in your control:

   - How you dress.
   - Who you choose to interact with.
   - Your attitude.
   - The effort you put in at work.
   - The effort you put in communicating with others.
   - The time you spend worrying.
   - Time you spend exercising.
   - How you deal with daily stress.

2. Work to reduce the extent to which you mentally and physically allow those pieces that you can't control to impact your life. Some examples are:

   - Concerns about how people interact with you.
   - Concerns about your future health.
   - Concerns about your future financial state.
   - Potential for unforeseen events to occur.
   - Your current boss at your current job.

3. Don't let unreasonable optimism or pessimism rule your life. Stay grounded in the notion that good and bad things will happen but they shouldn't change your day to day outlook.

Remember there are big pieces to your life over which you

direct the outcome and there are other areas that are outside your control. It's your responsibility to take time to understand which is which. And while you're at it, why not make it your goal to determine that good things will happen to you in threes and bad things will only happen in twos. Darn it, I just spilled my coffee on the new tablecloth. Well, one down one to go.

Wading Through the Pitfalls of Office Politics - Top Ten Pitfalls to Avoid

Some people would love to star in a TV reality show. But the workplace isn't the proper place to star in a reality show. To stay on track for job security and potential promotion you need to maintain the correct profile at work. You need to stay out of the daily drama that has the potential to swallow you up if you aren't on your guard. There are some common sense steps everyone should take to keep them out of the potential chaos of office politics. Here are my top ten:

1. Keep personal matters out of the work place. Gossip isn't a hobby you should take up. Keep conversations on business matters.

2. Make it your business to stay out of other people's business. Definitely show genuine concern about the workers in your workplace, without prying into others' personal matters.

3. Keep in mind that anything you say even in confidence can and may be told to anyone in the workplace. If you don't want information spread in the work place don't divulge it to anyone.

4. A work friend today may not be a work friend tomorrow. Relationships can change quickly, be prepared. Don't bare your soul if you don't want it potentially opened up to the entire workplace.

5. Keep a positive attitude. Perceptions about people are usually built in less than 60 seconds. Your positive attitude can deflect the potential for people to develop negative perceptions about you.

6. Always listen more than you talk. Avoid misunderstandings by first understanding the full extent of the issues being discussed. Remember once you've spoken it's public.

7. Don't be afraid to bring up business related topics or suggestions. You add individual value when you bring up quality information and ideas. Just make sure you present it in a clear unbiased manner so you don't offend other coworkers. Saying to your supervisor, "The shipping department is inefficient." is not clear and unbiased. Saying, "I've come across some interesting new shipping software that can streamline the shipping process. Can I provide you with more details? What do you think?" is clear and unbiased.

8. Don't talk about politics or other controversial issues at work. Religion, gun laws, or right to life issues should be kept off the discussion plate, unless they are part of what you do as part of your job description.

9. Be aware of people's space and don't over step their boundaries. Take time to get to know your coworkers to get a feel for what they want to talk about and what topics they consider to be personal and off limits. Each person has their own boundaries.

10. Always maintain professional decorum. Humor, joking and light conversation has its place in the workplace in moderation. Always make sure that comments aren't made that ridicule, demean or negatively affect another coworker.

Keep in mind that the work place is just that a place to get work done. Always maintain an air of professionalism, keep defined boundaries, and think before you disclose information to others. Save your personal persona for your day off.

Use Your Day Wisely

You only have so many hours in the day. You want to make sure you get time to drink that cup of coffee or that diet soda and have time for a mid morning break to see if there are any donuts or bagels left in the break room. Plus you don't want to still be at the office past midnight. You want to keep your life on track with a reasonable daily schedule. Here are some thoughts on using your day wisely so you don't have to stay on the treadmill all day long.

1. E-mail management. Don't become a slave to your e-mail account. Most people can waste up to half their day with an unorganized e-mail account. To start, leverage the management of your e-mail account by organizing it through your smart phone. For additional tips on organizing your e-mail account go to "Top 10 Tips for Keeping Your e-mail Inbox Clean"[14].

2. Organize using a planner. Figure out the most efficient way for you to track meetings, tasks and other events. Use what works best for you, but keep it simple. The system you develop, whether it's electronic, manual or a combination, must be one you will use and use consistently. Your smart phone is the best place to start. If you need an organizer app for your phone, go to "Twelve of the Best Calendar Apps Available for Your Android Smartphone Today"[15].

3. Organize your life. It's all about planning the day in advance. Sure things change quickly as the day gets going. But, start your day out with an outline of your

[14] http://www.computerhope.com/tips/tip88.htm
[15] http://thenextweb.com/apps/2013/08/16/12-of-the-best-calendar-apps-available-for-your-android-smartphone-today/

mind. Take a moment before you start your day to think through what you need to get accomplished. Write it down or save it in your smart phone.

4. Be realistic in what you can accomplish in a given time frame. You know what you can get done on a daily basis. Don't over commit yourself with appointments and projects that you have no hope of finishing. Balance out each day when scheduling in advance with the right mix of meetings and tasks that you will have the energy and focus to complete.

5. Manage your distractions appropriately. You know what level of distractions you can handle to successfully complete any task. Take time to eliminate distractions (hold calls, close doors, get out of the office) so you can focus on the task at hand.

6. Maintain antivirus and anti e-mail spam software. You don't want to think about it. Most offices have it covered on their work computers. If you are doing work at home, though, make sure you're covered there as well. An infected computer can really slow you down. Check with your IT person at work for suggest ions on what to do to cover your computer from viruses and e-mail spam. You can get more info at "The Best Tools for Removing Malware"[16]and "Spam Filters for Windows" [17].

7. Make sure to get breaks. You need a break to recharge your mind and refocus. A quick walk or a ten minute meditation session can be just the thing to get your mind back on track.

---

[16] http://betanews.com/2013/11/28/the-best-tools-for-removing-malware/
[17] http://download.cnet.com/windows/spam-filters/

8. Make sure to eat regularly. Don't skip meals. Starting off with breakfast you need to fuel up your body and mind to run efficiently throughout the day. Some thoughts on healthy eating can be found at "How to Eat Healthy"[18].

The sooner you make these changes the sooner you'll have a more organized and productive day. That should free up time to start that exercise routine you wanted to begin or give you extra time to relax at night with a good book, and a bowl of ice cream.

---

[18] http://www.fitness.gov/eat-healthy/how-to-eat-healthy/

Become You 2.0

Attitude is the key ingredient to create a consistent ability to succeed. You need to strive to improve yourself to "You 2.0", a person who works to reach a higher level each day. It isn't enough to win to succeed. Your goal shouldn't be how do I best those around me. You succeed by learning with each task you do or with each interaction you have with others. At the end of the day can you look back and say yes I learned something valuable, something new, today. I may not have closed that sale or finished that project but what did I learn about myself or about those that I came in contact with today. Ten steps I will try to do every day:

1. I will learn something new each day. The key to learning is maintaining an open mind.

2. I will apply something new I learned recently today.

3. I will take a step forward and not two steps back. If you're not learning you're not moving forward.

4. I will spend 5 minutes each day at the end of the day and ask myself what did I learn today.

5. When I go into a meeting or sales call that is similar to one I did previously, I will take the time to think about what I learned last time and apply it this time around.

6. I will remember that no two situations are ever the same, but I will focus on adapting, using the tools I have previously learned to meet the challenges of the new situation.

7. I will willingly accept the challenge to improve, always maintaining a positive attitude.

8. I will prepare myself to adapt to new situations.

9. I will use learning to expand my comfort zone, looking to learn about areas that I am not familiar.

10. What I learn I will share. By sharing you fine tune what you have learned and get used to including what you have learned in your daily routine.

Keep these ten simple ideas in your mind every day. They are the key to succeeding, to moving forward, to improving, to learning, to becoming You 2.0.

Are Expectations Controlling Your Life or Guiding Your Life?

Our lives are built on expectations. Everything we do on a day to day basis is in response to our expectations. We have expectations about everything, from people, to places to things. Based on our expectations, when we do something, we believe a certain chain of events will occur. But how reasonable are our expectations? And can we really measure the reasonableness of our expectations? There are some things to think about when weighing how reasonable our expectations are:

1. The focus of our expectations isn't just limited to us individually. We have expectations of others as well. We need to understand the limitations of the expectations we have of others. Our control over others is extremely limited.

2. We may have an expectation that we can control others' actions, but in reality we have no control over others' actions.

3. When we're just dealing with ourselves we can be pretty assured of what will ultimately happen. However, we never move in an isolated vacuum. Keep in mind that our expectations are just that, expectations, be prepared that they may need to change. Be open to changing expectations.

4. Don't get hung up on how you expect others might respond. Worrying about other people's responses becomes a needless waste of energy. When we throw others into the equation the variables become many and the outcomes almost infinite. We can't plan for infinite outcomes.

5. When we interact with someone, don't automatically expect them to respond in the same way we would. Many times we are at a loss when someone does something totally different then what we would do. Bottom line is we need to accept the fact that people won't always respond in the manner we anticipate.

6. Instead of being resentful or getting upset when our expectations aren't met, we should focus our energy on understanding why the expectation wasn't met. Again focus on weighing whether or not the expectations were reasonable. If not, why not.

7. When a person's response doesn't meet our expectations don't take it personally. Expectations shouldn't be etched in stone give them room to grow and change.

8. Do stay unemotional and rational with expectations. Expectations should be treated as a tool we can use, not a character flaw that we should latch onto at all costs.

9. We should set expectations based on actual facts. We can dream, but know that difference between reality and dreams. Stay grounded in reality when setting expectations.

10. Base expectations on the most likely outcome, but realize that probability isn't the same as certainty.

We all have expectations. But expectations shouldn't take control of our lives. We need to continually assess whether our expectations are reasonable, that we use them as a tool to reduce our stress, and let them help us predict the outcomes of situations. If that's not happening we need to reassess the reasonableness of our expectations.

Staying Current in a World of Change

We all refer to today as the information age. More correctly it should be called the age of change. Changes in technology are happening daily and trends are rising and falling quickly. We feel stretched to stay current with it all. We continually need to stay on top of the learning curve to make sure we know about the most recent trends and latest technology. Today's news grows old quickly and is replaced by new news throughout the day. Everything is happening at a rapid pace. So how do we even attempt to stay on top of all the information.

1. Don't try to juggle and absorb every type of social media. Do your research and stay current with a few types of social media that you feel comfortable using on a regular basis. Better to use a few types of social media well than to do many poorly. LinkedIn for business; Facebook for trends and personal information; and then chose Pinterest, Instagram, or Tumblr for more video based interaction.

2. Unless you're the ultimate trend setter, don't feel compelled to ride each new trend. Stay with your current systems until you find that they are holding you back. Be willing to embrace new technologies, but after they become mainstream.

3. Pick one or two news providers. I find quick apps on your phone work best. You can quickly access the day's news a few times during the day. Some of note:

   a. Google News - free

   b. Your local newspaper internet version - sometimes

you have to subscribe to get all the articles.

c. Fox News - free

d. CNN - free

e. Yahoo News - free

Note that every news provider has its own biases, so pick the one you're most comfortable with.

4. As the number of people using social media has exploded the response time it takes to get back to people using media has lagged. Keep in mind that it is more important to keep a timely dialogue going with friends and potential customers than it is to keep a broadcast on your social media current. Communication is a two way street. Make sure you're responding to people in a timely manner.

5. Less can be more productive. Don't get bogged down in complex technology systems that you know you won't use on a regular basis. Only use technology you feel comfortable using or are will to take steps to learn to use correctly.

6. The better organized you are the more current you can stay on top of changing events. Use different technologies to supplement one another. Maybe use your mobile device for pure texting of simple responses on your work or personal e-mail account and to check news updates. Use your tablet or laptop for responding to more complex work e-mails and to work on work projects. If you still use a desk top save that for more complex projects that might require multiple screens, programs and documents.

7. Maximize productivity by syncing all of your files to every

device. Consider using services like:

a. Dropbox;

b. iCloud; or

c. Google Drive.

To store your files on the Cloud.

Remember with a fast paced work and social environment, chaos is always a step away. You need to stay organized to stay productive. Stay current in a world of change.

Mistakes Happen - How You Deal With Those Mistakes Makes the Difference

Yes, mistakes happen in our business and personal lives; none of us is perfect. How we respond when those mistakes happen, however, can determine how quickly we recover, learn and move on from those mistakes. Assessing how the mistake was made will help us avoid a similar mistake in the future; and if we understand how to work through the mistake cleanup process, any problems caused by the mistake can be minimized.

I think mistakes fall into two categories:

1. Mistakes made due to inexperience. These mistakes sometimes can't be avoided. People can make mistakes because they lack critical knowledge to make the right decision. Once the mistake is made make sure to learn from it. Gain additional knowledge so that you're prepared the next time. The only thing worse than making a mistake is making the same mistake twice.

2. Mistakes made due to lack of focus. These mistakes are more difficult to assess. These are mistakes are normally made by a seasoned experienced person. The important step to take is to look at the mistake and positively review how it happened. The goal here is to understand how the mistake occurred:

   a. Were you moving too quickly?
   b. Were you distracted?
   c. Did you not look at all the facts?
   d. Were you too self assured?
   e. Did you cut corners?

Take a look at what caused the mistake and then take a moment to figure out what can be done to change current patterns or behavior so it doesn't happen again. If need be, write down the mistake made and the corrective steps you plan on taking in the future to avoid similar mistakes.

Once you've determined how the mistake occurred, then you need to begin cleanup mode.

1. Understand how people respond to and handle mistakes. This prepares you for working with others when mistakes are made. I categorize people into three basic groups, when it comes to how people handle mistakes. But keep in mind that these are very broad groups. Each person has their own age, educational, generational, and personal life experience differences that affect how they deal with mistakes. The basic groups are:

   a.   Extroverts. They want to get everything out in the open. They will talk about the problem to try to get it resolved. While talking it through they may not initially have all of the facts to resolve the problem. For them discussion is all part of the resolution process.

   b.   Analytical people. They tend to work through in their mind the cleanup process. They try to come up with a solution before presenting their concerns. Will wait until they have all facts and possible solutions before communicating to others about the existence of a mistake.

   c.   Introverts. They may keep it bottled up and not tell others hoping it will go away. Fear can drive them to not face and take the steps necessary to remedy the mistake. Can be concerned about being blamed or criticized for the mistake.

2. Take the proper cleanup steps to deal with a mistake:

   a. Don't Procrastinate. Deal with the mistake

immediately. The longer you take to respond the greater the possibility of more harm.

b. Gather all the facts. Make sure you get all the facts. Understand the scope of the mistake and what exactly happened.

c. Don't be ruled by fear of criticism or blame. No one likes to be blamed or criticized. When mistakes happen, blame and criticism should be removed from the cleanup process. Don't allow the potential for blame or criticism to lead you to inaction.

d. After you have gathered all the facts put together a plan of action to remedy the mistake. The plan should include communicating to people that need to know, that the mistake has occurred and how it is being corrected.. Share the mistake and possible solutions with at least one other trusted coworker or friend. This provides you with an advice outlet and covers you if additional problems arise.

3. Complete the mistake cleanup process in a positive manner. Properly handling a mistake is as important as avoiding the mistake the next time around. Look closely at how you and those around you deal with mistakes. Different types of people handle the mistake cleanup process in different ways. Think about the best way to handle the cleanup process based on the people that are involved. Review the process you used   and note whether it worked well and if there are any changes that should be made in the process the next time around.

Everyone makes mistakes. Don't create a bigger mistake by thinking that you're the only one to make them. Take proactive steps to clean up the mistake in a positive timely manner. Learn from your mistakes and then move on.

Do Rituals Rule Our Lives?

We all have our rituals that we stick to on a daily, weekly or other set basis. Some are quirky things we do individually and others are more elaborate routines we go through with others. There are religious, social, and group based rituals. There are individual rituals like combing our hair a certain number of times each morning, putting a lucky coin or memento in our pocket, or taking the same path to work each day. Some of us follow more rituals than others. But, our lives are filled with them; they weave their way throughout our lives. Why are they so important to us?

1.   Rituals add meaning to our lives. They provide us with a regular reminder of those things that are important in our lives. Even though they may seem insignificant when we do them, the fact that we continue to them makes them important.

2.   Rituals reduce chaos in our lives. For a brief moment the process of the ritual has a calming effect. Our focus is drawn to the matter at hand instead of the many other things going on in our life. For a short moment we have held back the chaos that surrounds us.

3.   Rituals create consistency. We become grounded in the repetition of these small or elaborate processes. It is within the process that we train ourselves to perceive and work through patterns. Many patterns continually recur in what we do. The consistency in how we respond to those same patterns helps us be more even centered individually.

4.   Rituals help us solidify expectations. In the process of completing rituals we have an exact sequence of events that we are completing. We are in fact rebuilding basic blocks in the foundation of our lives. Each ritual we complete reaffirms these basic building blocks.

5.   Rituals give us mind at peace. We find Peace and tranquility by completing a simple set of tasks that give us a sense of simple accomplishment. It is the act of completing something that gives us comfort in the midst of always having to deal with more complex daily problems.

Rituals are important as a way to ground us and shape our daily lives. But, there are times when we should pause to think about the rituals we perform and decide whether or not they help or detract from our daily living. In the end healthy rituals improve healthy lives.

A Good Employee - The Right Fit at the Right Time

What makes individuals good employees? There are numerous answers to this question. Both employees and employers have differing ideas on what is most important though. If you ask people the answers vary from productivity, to number of sales, to meeting annual goals, to getting along with fellow employees. Yes these all come into play in determining whether an employee is a keeper. The important things worth looking at, really focus on a full past, present and future review of the employee.

1. Has the employee met the prior year's individual goals. A motivated employee meets or exceeds prior year goals. If the employee isn't doing that, look at what is holding the employee back from meeting them. If it is the employee's fault and not outside circumstances, then the employee might not be the best fit for that job.

2. Has the employee helped improve the company. Where has an employee furthered the broader company goals. This shows whether the employee understands the needs of the company and has a desire to see the company succeed.

3. Does the employee strive to meet annual goals. Is the employee motivated and driven. Goals should be set at the beginning of the year and should be discussed and agreed to by both employee and supervisor. Usually it's good to have employee draft initial goals. Always keep the goals realistic but challenging.

4. Does the employee fit the company's personality. Every

company has a culture, a personality all its own. An employee needs to fit within that culture. Size and type of company all make a difference on what type of person might be a good fit.

5. Does the employee work positively with those around him or her. Ability of a person to interact well with others keeps the positive energy of the company intact. Negative people detract from the positive direction of the company.

6. Does the employee move forward the vision of the company. Individuals have their own goals and ideas. Make sure those are in sync with the direction the company plans on taking.

7. Are the employee's talents being utilized. If not, why not. If an employee's talents aren't going to be needed in the future, now might be the time to cut ties with the employee rather than allowing the employee's dissatisfaction with under utilization of his or her skills affect other employees' morale or the focus of the company.

8. Does the employee fit in the future plans of the company. The company has a specific direction that it is planning to take through its strategic plan . The company should make sure an employee's skills, knowledge, and expertise fit those short and long term plans.

9. Is the employee a valuable resource for the company. A company needs to continually assess whether the value, both tangible and intangible skills, expertise, and knowledge, an employee brings to the company outweighs the salary, insurance, and other costs that the company pays out to the

employee.

10. What are the employee's broader personal goals. Any review of an employee's goals should include the question - "Where do you see yourself in five years?" Supervisors should add it to their yearly reviews. Understanding where someone wants to be in the future, is the best way to see where those goals fit in with the company's goals for growth and improvement. If they mesh that's great, if not, take a look a look at where they differ and if they can be made to sync up with the company's goals.

Good employees aren't just found, they aren't a fixed commodity. They change and develop over time. As the needs and focus of the company change, the need for certain types of employees change. Over time some employees become a better fit while others lose their fit within the company altogether. Being a good employee is all about fitting in the right company at the right time.

What's to Worry About

We all worry about different things in our lives. For most of us worry is just a small part of our busy daily lives. For some of us, though, worry can impair our decision making abilities. Fear of what may or may not happen or fear of the consequences of making a wrong decision can begin to hamper our ability to handle decision making properly. Some worry is good because it helps us focus on how we should make certain decisions to avoid negative outcomes in our lives. Some worry keeps us vigilant to look out for and be prepared for the occurrence of certain events. But if we worry about too much in our life or if we spend too much of our time worrying about what may or may not happen, then worry begins to become unhealthy, it can take over our lives. Here are some things to think about when dealing with worry.

1.   Remember 99 percent of what you worry about doesn't eventually occur. Filter out the improbable. Focus on the one percent that is most likely to occur.

2.   Only spend a limited amount of time thinking about concerns you might have on any one issue. If you have an idea of what might happen, write it down and then note what options you can take to deal with the issue if it does happen. If you start beginning to worry about it again, review your notes to assure yourself you have already decided the best way to handle the situation. Make changes as necessary to your solution as facts or circumstances change.

3.   Think about what is at the root of your worrying. Is there a common thread or theme that weaves through your worries. For example if you worry more about

financial problems than anything else, take some proactive steps to improve your finances to reduce your overall worry.

4.   Unless facts in your life change don't fixate on the potential for a certain event to occur. The likelihood of something happening only changes if the facts change. Train yourself to adapt your mental focus to the most immediate issues that need your attention. Worrying about issues that are not yet ripe for you to make a decision, is just a waste of your energy.

5.   Don't get stuck in a worry loop. Develop outlets like reading, conversation with close friends, or exercise to help you filter out the worry and help you move on to another thought process.

Extended worry can consume a lot of energy and over time wear you down both physically and mentally. Stay sharp by getting enough rest, eating healthy and focusing on those things in your life that you can control. Remember, worrying about layers of uncertain events is unproductive. Worrying about things that may likely impact you in the near future helps you stay focused and can lead you along the proper decision making path.

Finesse Equals Success

No one likes a bull in their china shop. But, everyone likes a person that makes them feel at peace, at ease with themselves. This is true even when you know that person is working to get what they want. People are more receptive to work with you, if you develop your own style of finesse when dealing with people and situations. Finesse will take you to a higher level of success. What is the art of finesse all about?

1. It's about thinking before acting. Don't act impulsively. Weigh out your thoughts before you turn them into actions.

2. Being subtle yet focused. You don't need to be pushy to get your point across.

3. Being artful in the way you handle people and situations. Craft the way you approach people and situations. Think about unique ways to approach people and situations. Keep in mind one approach doesn't work for everyone or for every situation.

4. Being self assured, but with a sense of purpose. Be confident in how you approach things. But always make sure that confidence is moving you in a positive well thought out direction.

5. Being patient. Know that some things take longer than others to be successfully completed. Don't force things to occur when the time isn't right.

6. Being strategic in how you handle situations. Lay out the steps to handle a situation in your mind ahead of time.

7. Being methodical. It's OK to move slowly. Be measured

in your thought process and in how you talk about your ideas. Speaking about or moving your agenda too quickly can cause people to react negatively.

8. Creating a buffer in dealing with people. Don't let people get to you mentally. Responses from others shouldn't be taken personally. Most often, their responses are for their benefit not yours. Always keep that in mind.

9. Getting what you want out of a situation, but not at the expense of the other person. Always be mindful of the big picture. It isn't about a successful outcome to one situation, it's about a successful outcome that builds a long term relationship.

10. Being prepared in your mind for situations before they occur. Think about a plan of action in advance. Don't assume things will always occur in a specific manner.

Create your own unique art form, a more defined personality. You can't be perfect, but you can improve by crafting the life you live with finesse. Be a person with added substance, add finesse to improve your success.

Did Dinosaurs Have Souls?

It only seems we think outside the box when we are faced with a unique problem; one that needs to be solved using tools we normally don't rely on. Take, for example, the philosophical question, "Did dinosaurs have souls?" Forget about the historical or religious implications of this question. I'm sure few of us have had any experience on this topic.

In our lives, from time to time we come across unique problems that need to be solved. We need to be prepared to look at things differently to analyze these issues. It's something outside of the ordinary sphere of most people's expertise. But, why should we limit thinking outside the box to only those out of the ordinary situations?

Thinking outside the box can be a good exercise in developing problem solving skills. We can consistently use it as a tool to come up with better solutions. Too often we get entrenched in doing things the same way and don't challenge ourselves to look at things from a unique perspective. A change in perspective can lead us to solve problems in a new way, leading us to better outcomes. How can we strive to think outside the box?

1.   The initial discussion phase. Open dialogue should initially allow for a free flow of ideas. Put together a brainstorming group and hash over the issue. It is sometimes only when we begin the dialogue that we realize the different perspectives from which a problem can be analyzed.

2.   Think about where you start your problem solving analysis. Are you truly starting at the beginning or are you taking for granted that certain procedures must

occur. Make sure you are truly looking at things from the starting point.

3.   The thinking process is key. Not everything that you think about is worth pursuing, but by verbalizing thoughts you put the thought process in motion. One random idea can lead to another idea and so on until you reach something more concrete. Don't be afraid to verbalize an idea, even one that is strange; it may be useful in your quest to a solution to your problem.

4.   Limit the randomness. Focus on your ultimate purpose of reaching a solution to your problem. You need to set a time limit and choose a group moderator who is skilled at bringing discussion back to the matter at hand. But the moderator should give the group some latitude in the discussions, time permitting.

5.   Exercise your own abilities to think outside your thought box. Exercises you can do.
   a. Go somewhere you've never gone before and think about your experience.
   b. Talk to five new people you've never talked to before and take time to listen to their viewpoints on a specific topic.
   c. Write down randomly your most strange solutions to something that you come across daily. Review it a week later.

We may not have to solve the age old question of whether dinosaurs had souls, but we will encounter difficult problems in our personal or business lives, that will need to be solved. When we work to develop our skill to "think outside the box" we make ourselves better problem solvers for those difficult problems we do encounter. Are you prepared to think outside the box?

Ever Try Some "People Centric" Behavior?

You can expand the world around you by becoming "people centric" instead of "me centric"; and you can learn a thing or two about human nature in the process. Most people consistently focus on what is going on in their own lives. They just think about everything from their perspective. They become oblivious to what's going on in the lives of the people around them. Take time to get to know the people around you. Taking time to understand what is going on with the people you come in contact with everyday, can improve your ability to understand the people around you and in the end better understand yourself.

1. Don't deal with people generically, deal with them individually. Think about it, no two people are alike. Why are you interacting with the people you do? You choose to interact with one another because of each other's unique qualities. So treat each person as an individual and deal with each person on an individual specific basis.

2. Take time to read people. Take a moment to assess people. What is their current attitude? What is their emotional state? Think about what might be on their mind. Meet them in their state of mind rather than in yours.

3. Take the time to get to know people. It all starts by listening; and also asking some specific questions about them.

4. If you meet in their office or their house take the time to get to know their surroundings. Get a feel for what they are all about; what are their interests; and what are their tastes. You aren't snooping you're showing an interest in what they are putting on public display.

5. Assess what is important to them. Think about what things they want to talk about. Sometimes letting the conversation drift allows the other person to direct the conversation. See where the conversation goes and what topics they choose to discuss.

6. How do they interact with you and others? Take notice of how people interact with others, from clerks to other acquaintances, to coworkers. How people interact with different types of people will tell you a lot about their character.

7. Follow up with the next meeting by showing interest in something you learned about the person from the first meeting. Ask about a vacation they just got back from, an event they attended, or a mutual acquaintance.

8. Don't be superficial. Your interest in others has to be real. If you don't interact with others on a real, energetic in depth basis, they will likely stop taking the time and energy to do the same with you.

Moving outside your "me centric" world requires a little time and energy. In the end though, you get to know more about the people around you and yourself as well. Try out some "people centric" behavior, you might learn something new.

Where's Your Moral Compass

It's easy to get lost in the quagmire of day to day business dealings. We're all struggling to get new business, make new sales, complete our daily job tasks, or work at maintaining our value to our boss and our company. We may begin to stop thinking about what we are doing or why we are doing it. That's when we need to reassess our moral direction. At what cost can we afford to step outside the correct setting of our moral compass to complete our business goals. Think about steps you need to take to maintain your moral compass setting.

1.   If someone asks you to do something that doesn't seem right odds are it isn't. Don't do it. This may seem like simple advice, but most often your own instincts can keep you on the right track; you just need to listen to your instincts.

2.   You're not just as good as your last sale or last task completed; you're only as good as the ethics you used to get your last sale or last task completed. Remember the relationship created by a sale or completed task is more important than the sale or task. The sale or task is a onetime event the relationship created through the sale or task process is a lifetime event.

3.   You work for a lifetime don't screw up a life time of work by one poor decision. We all make mistakes, but don't go out of your way to do something you know isn't right. Most people can forgive mistakes, but most people don't forget being treated poorly on purpose.

4.Other people's willingness to work with you hinges on their ability to trust you. Trust is hard to build. Once it is lost it is difficult if not impossible to rebuild. Building trust with others should always be one of your top priorities.

5.   Don't go blindly into things. Be willing to ask questions even from supervisors or managers to make sure you understand what is being asked of you and why.

6. Always take the high road. Don't get caught in a battle of negative ethics. In the end you rarely win. There are certain people that aren't worth doing business with. It may seem difficult to disengage from ethically challenged people early on, but it will save you from more problems in the future.

7.   If a boss or manager asks you to handle something for them that is their duty to do, think twice about handling it without a full understanding of why they are unwilling to do it.

8.   Find a good mentor. Have someone you trust who you can use as a sounding board. If you have concerns about something run it past this person. Don't be afraid to ask for advice.

Keeping your moral compass directed in the right direction will serve you well in whatever direction your life takes you. Always take a moment to look at your moral compass and adjust your direction as needed.

Take Time To Challenge Your Life

Many times we allow ourselves to settle into the simplicity of our day to day lives or we simply grow bored with the mundane existence we lead. Sometimes where we are in life is where we want to be. But wherever we are in our lives, we shouldn't be simply going through the motions of living or working or whatever else it is we do on a day to day basis. If we don't find our life challenging, then it's time to challenge our life. We shouldn't just sit back and accept our current situation. There are steps we can take to challenge our life.

1.Don't be afraid to try something new. For example, if you have a desire to do ballroom dancing, start with some lessons. Never let the fact that you aren't good at something or don't know how to do something stop you from pursuing it.

2.   Stop going through the motions. If you don't like what you are doing figure out a timeframe to make a change. Doing something that you don't like doing, even if you are good at it won't make you happy. In fact if will keep you from what will make you happy.

3.   Never say I'm too busy to make a change. If you're busy and unhappy with your current situation you still need to find some time to make change in your life. You should change your priorities so you can start moving in a direction that puts you into a happier lifestyle.

4.   You need to find a niche in your life that you are passionate about. Write down what it is that you most want to do. Then figure out how you can incorporate it into your day to day routine. If you like music, you may not become a full time musician over night but you can join a choir, join a

band, or just make a point of going to a concert once a week or once a month.

5.   Don't just say "I'm unhappy where I am right now" without being willing to take steps to change. Only you control whether change in your life will occur. If you say you're unhappy where you are right now, you've already taken the first step. Don't stop there; take the next steps to actually change.

6.   Add substance to your life. So many people fall for get rich quick schemes because those schemes offer us something that is missing in our own lives. The schemes give us something to dream about and something to feel passionate about, seemingly, without any effort on our part. Don't let someone else profit at your expense, from your own need to dream and feel passionate about something. Invest some time in yourself, infuse your own passion and dreams in your life, and don't let others try to do it for you.

We shouldn't just go through the motions of life. We should strive to live our lives with substance. Find what motivates you. Many of us settle for something less because we are unwilling to rise up and challenge ourselves by taking on something new in our lives. Are you willing to challenge your life?

Spend a Weekend Reaching for Relaxation

Today there are so many things that keep our lives busy and stressful. Continually we are moving at a fast pace; technology forces us to move at an even faster one. We juggle appointments, work and family matters nonstop. Why not take some time to just grab some "me" time? Why not try to reach for some ultimate relaxation? It really isn't that difficult and afterwards you'll feel refreshed and ready to take on a new week. Give it a try, a weekend of stress free bliss awaits. These are the simple steps to take:

1. Before the weekend begins stock up your refrigerator. Mix up your food choices with a few decadent items, but also some healthy alternatives. Go for some items you normally don't buy. Do your shopping after a meal so you don't go too crazy.

2. Turn off you cell phone and put it in a drawer for the entire weekend. Don't even give in to the temptation of checking it for messages.

3. Unplug the land line phone or turn the ringer off. Truthfully most calls you get anyway are from political candidates or companies looking for donations.

4. Turn off your computer or ipad and put it away. This might be difficult if you're an internet junkie. But avoid the temptation to turn it on. Your goal should be to limit exposure to the outside world.

5. Turn off the TV. The goal is not to be distracted by

advertising or the outside world. If you want to watch something, limit it to an old DVD movie you have around the house or keep it old school and rent one. They still have red boxes around town. The goal is to limit your ability to be negatively distracted by ads or current events. Remove all clocks. Don't let time dictate what you think you should be doing. Just do what comes to mind when it comes to mind.

6. Find a quiet place to sit in your house or apartment. There might be more than one place you can find that is comfortable. Just take in your surroundings and enjoy the simple sounds and view. As you get more relaxed with just being with yourself, you'll find you can sit longer.

7. Now get to the important things to aid in relaxation:

> a. Take a long walk.
> b. Take a nap.
> c. Cook something you normally don't cook.
> d. Sit down with a good book.
> e. Write down your thoughts and ideas.
> f. Watch that old movie you've wanted to see but haven't found the time to watch.
> g. Any other quiet "me" time that you find relaxing.

At the end of the weekend, write down your thoughts; jot down what you thought of the experience, positives and negatives. Was it an enjoyable experience? Make plans for your next weekend of relaxation.

Let Laughter Rule Your Day

As the Joker said, "Why so serious?" When he says that phrase we wonder what sinister thoughts and deeds come along with the laughter. His tone is ominous and foreboding; he's taunting us to our core. Seriously though, why do we have to be so concerned about adding laughter into our life? Sure we have to be serious enough to work to pay the bills, provide for our families and strive to accomplish our goals. But, a little laughter, for that matter, a lot of laughter in your life makes life more enjoyable. Most of us tend to be serious from the moment we wake up until we go to bed. Why not try for one full day, to infuse a little laughter in it.

1.   Begin your day with a laugh. Think about something funny. Then just try to start laughing. See if you feel more relaxed and in a better mood, after your laugh. If you can't laugh at least smile at yourself in the mirror.

2.   Laugh with someone during the day. Find someone you can share a funny story or joke with. See if you can share a moment of laughter together. Does it make you feel closer to that person? Do you feel more comfortable interacting with that person now?

3.   Laugh with yourself. You don't need to laugh "at" yourself. Laugh with yourself about something during the day that seems funny to you. Does that make you feel more comfortable with yourself; more confident acknowledging something funny that you hadn't previous thought about?

4.   Find something humorous in what you do. Look at yourself and find something humorous in your daily tasks or life. Laugh or at least break a little smile about what it is you do that makes you laugh. Does this give some new meaning to your life or make you question what changes might help improve your life?

5.   End your day with a laugh. Round out the end of your day with a little laughter. Think back and see if there isn't some humor that you've found along the way that comes to mind. Then, stand in front of the mirror and laugh.

See you went through an entire day creating laughter as you went. Didn't that make your day more enjoyable? Now try it on a daily basis. You'll find that you'll look forward to each new day a little differently; and find it a challenge to make someone else laugh during the day too. Just make sure to infuse the proper amount of seriousness as needed.

Who's Keeping Time Anyway?

Everyone has their own perception of
what is timely. Maybe it's because we all
have a unique internal clock. Some of us
have our own internal clock that runs like a
finely tuned Swiss watch; for others when
they decide they're good and ready is
when they show up for an event or
meeting; and then for others still it's a
mix depending on their mood that day.
When it comes to different situations people should be aware
of what is the "time" norm and what is each individual's need
and/or desire when it comes to dealing with time. Here are
some things to think about with timeliness.

1. Responding to social media. Social media moves and
   changes quickly. If you want to be relevant and current
   with the message dialogue then you need to do a quick
   turnaround with you r response. But always be aware
   that sometimes people put info out there not necessarily
   for a response or to start a dialogue, but to simply
   make a statement; in that case you may be hard pressed
   to get a timely response or a response at all for that
   matter. Your response then, becomes a simple
   acknowledgement to the writer that you've seen the
   posting. In that instance time isn't important.

2. Attending a business meeting. Always be a few minutes
   early. That way you can size up your surroundings and
   feel relaxed and confident when the meeting starts.
   Depending on the meeting location, you also pick the
   most comfortable spot or most advantageous seat at
   the table. Also, you'd rather have the other person

apologize to you for being late than you apologizing to them for being late.

3. Attending a party. Unless it's a sit down dinner set for a specific time, you can always feel free to come a few minutes late or when you're good and ready. Keep in mind though people do remember those who arrive early and those who arrive late.

4. Responding to mailed info. The nature of mail suggests that the person who sent you the mail isn't in a rush for a response. Mailed info can allow you a little extra time to get your response out. But don't be rude and forget to respond altogether; and always respond by a response request date provided in the correspondence.

5. Business responses. When it comes to business it isn't about your time frame. You need to respond on your customer's time frame or schedule. Understand what their expectations are in terms of a response time. Respond in the same manner that your customer initially contacted you unless your response requires a different message medium. For example an e-mail message should be responded with an e-mail message.

6. Personal responses. Responses to personal messages are more on your time. But if you want to keep those relationships in good order don't wait too long to respond.

7. Be aware of a person's "time" cues. If you aren't sure how much time a person has for a meeting or when they expect a response, ask them. Otherwise listen to them for hints about their personal time clock. Remember rigidly punctual people have less tolerance for

mismanagement of time, whereas people who aren't as time sensitive are more open to liberal use of time.

8. Take control of time as needed. Don't be afraid to manage time usage as you see fit. Don't be afraid to speak your mind and let others know you have limited time to meet or to talk. People will respect you more in the long run for being open with them.

Timeliness is really relative from one person to another. You can really set your own rules on how quickly you respond or when you arrive. But keep in mind that others also have expectations. So make sure to sync your time clock with others when needed.

What's It Like Being Lucky?

I never thought of myself as being lucky. Some people say that they're inherently lucky; others just shake their head and say "I have no luck whatsoever. Those "unlucky" people look around themselves and think everyone else is getting all the luck, shouldn't they get lucky sometime. Luck isn't really about whether or not it follows one person or another. No luck is all about perception and attitude.

1. If you think you'll be lucky you are. Positive thinking changes your mindset and allows you to notice those moments when things work out. Those minor accomplishments may not be that big win, but allow yourself to recognize and enjoy the moment when you have a small triumph in your life.

2. Focus on the positive things that happen to you, not the negative. Luck isn't about things happening it's about you recalling how things happen. You won't be lucky if you only focus on the bad things that happen to you. If you only focus on the good things that happen to you, you'll be lucky all the time.

3. Don't dwell on others. Focusing on others, changes how you make decisions in your life. Instead, focus on yourself. Others aren't living your life, don't let what happens to them determine how you will make decisions in your own life. If you focus on what is happening to you on a daily

basis, you will hit on those opportunities that may have in the past passed you by unnoticed.

4. Don't become superstitious. Luck has historically been tied to superstition. However, most things happen for a reason. Trust in your own ability to make decisions. Don't limit the paths you take because of superstitious beliefs.

5. Market yourself. You are the one that best knows what you have to offer, what are the strengths you bring to the table. If you let people know you have a lucky attitude that might wear off on them, you increase the potential that more luck will come your way.

6. Don't take outrageous chances on things. Be reasonable in your choices. Take those chances that have a reasonable chance of success.

7.Being lucky is about being skillful in your choices. Think about the actions you take. Don't jump into something without taking a moment to think about how it may or may not play out.

Being lucky isn't about chance, it's about being skilled enough to focus on the positives in your life and live each day with confidence. You build luck when you choose to interact with your world in a positive thoughtful manner. See you have seven things to focus on now, isn't that lucky.

Business Etiquette in the Technology Age

Sure, staying connected through technology is important. However, many times we find our- selves a slave to our iPads, smart phones and computers. It's easy to get away from our[1]

number one priority, people. We can easily offend people in a business setting when we focus on our techno gadgets rather than the people we are actually communicating with through those gadgets. Proper etiquette can help maintain and build those personal connections, allowing us to stay 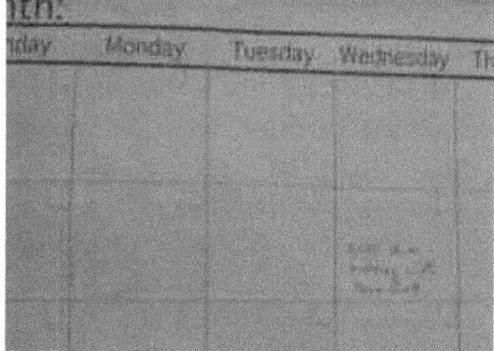 connected on a more personal level. Here are some thoughts on etiquette that can help you balance your reliance on technology with the importance of focusing your attention on the people around you.

1. Focus on people when meeting face to face. In a face to face meeting don't interrupt the meeting to answer your phone or check your messages, they can wait. Focus on the meeting at hand. Also, make sure to turn off your computer and phone devices when you head into a meeting. A constantly changing computer screensaver, or a tweeting or vibrating device can become annoying quickly.

2. Always double check the wording in instant messages and e-mails. All caps is always a no-no. Also subtle wordy messages may make your response come off as confusing or too demanding. Short answers may come

off as terse. The bottom line is:

a. Make sure you know your audience;

b. Take a moment to reread your message before you send it;

c. Remember people can't see your face when they read electronic messages all they have are your words and their current mood to go with it;

d. Choose your mode of communication wisely. A complex topic that is best discussed in person shouldn't be done via e-mail or instant messaging; and

e. Take a few extra moments to add explanatory words like "This is what I suggest" or "Let's discuss if you have concerns" to allow the recipient to request clarification.

3. Spelling is still important. In all correspondence - messaging, e-mailing, and written letters, make sure to spell words correctly. Limit your use of texting abbreviations like "ttyl", "bion", or "lol". Not everyone knows what they mean or appreciates when they're used. Make sure to spell the name of the person you are communicating with correctly. No one likes to get a generic response filled with abbreviations and with their name spelled wrong.

4. Mode of communication matters. With so many ways to get a hold of people, let people know which way is the best way to get a hold of you and likewise respect others' wishes by contacting them in the media they like best – e-mail, phone, instant messaging, etc. Not only will this simplify the communication process, you will probably get a quicker response.

5. There's a time and place for multitasking. Make sure your technology is safely stored away before interacting with people. This means stop typing on the computer or checking messages when you're on the phone and remove your phone ear piece before you go into meetings. People can tell when you're distracted and not focusing on the discussion at hand.

6. Make a point of listening. With so many distractions from the fast paced world we live in you will stand above the rest and be noticed if you pay attention and take in what the other person has to say. This includes in person and reading written messages. Always take an extra few minutes to read e-mail and text messages so you understand the full meaning of what is being said. Don't just read the first sentence. When meeting in person, give the person full eye contact and let them finish their thought process before responding.

Today we have more options in how we communicate with one another than ever before. We need to be respectful of others, connect with them in the manner they wish, focus our attention on them when we meet with them personally, and communicate in a thoughtful manner. Yes proper etiquette still matters.

www.ingramcontent.com/pod-product-compliance
Lightning Source LLC
Chambersburg PA
CBHW071725170526
45165CB00005B/2155